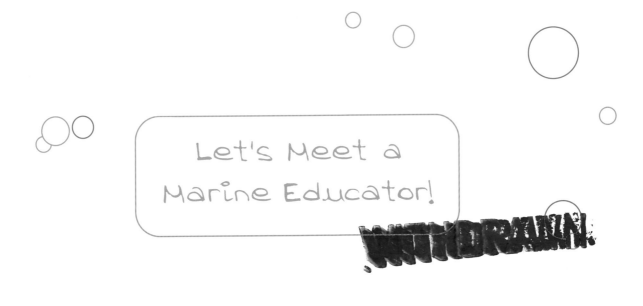

Let's Meet a Marine Educator!

By Tasha Jacobson

Windward Publishing
AN IMPRINT OF FINNEY COMPANY

Let's Meet a Marine Educator!
By Tasha Jacobson

ISBN-13: 978-0-89317-066-0

Cover images courtesy of Tammy Rach,
Dolphin Quest, Jessica Aschettino, Island
Life Photography, PhotoDisc, Inc., and
Robyn Larkin.

Designed by Angela Wix
Edited by Lindsey Cunneen

Windward Publishing
AN IMPRINT OF FINNEY COMPANY
8075 215th Street West
Lakeville, Minnesota 55044
www.finneyco.com

Printed in China
1 3 5 7 9 10 8 6 4 2

To Tammy, who constantly amazes me.
And to Alex, a beautiful blessing.

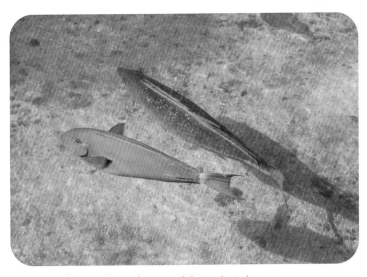

A surgeonfish and a jack enjoy life in their lagoon.
Photo courtesy of Tammy Rach

Tammy watching a sea lion swimming at the Aquarium of the Pacific.
Photo courtesy of Tammy Rach

Marine Educators

If you enjoy helping others learn, and you find the plants and animals of the sea amazing, you might want to become a marine educator.

Sea lions having a dock party.
Photo courtesy of Jessica Aschettino, Island Life Photography

A stinging catfish exhibit, including live corals and sea urchins.
Photo courtesy of Tammy Rach

A yellow tang at the Dolphin Quest lagoon.
Photo courtesy of Tammy Rach

What IS a Marine Educator?

Marine educators are professionals who teach others about marine life: plants and animals that live in the sea or ocean. They help others learn about ocean life by creating programs, teaching classes, giving presentations and tours, and more.

Ka'ena Point West, on the Island of Oahu.
Photo courtesy of Tammy Rach

Tammy Rach, a marine educator, teaching an outreach class about animal movement.
Photo courtesy of Dolphin Quest

Marine Plants and Animals

These educators teach about a variety of marine life, including: seals, sea lions, walruses, whales (including dolphins and porpoises), manatees, sea otters, eels, stingrays, octopuses, sea stars, reef fish, sea turtles, sea jellies, lobsters, crabs, coral, algae, kelp, and many other species.

Monk seal mother and pup resting on the beach.
Photo courtesy of Jessica Aschettino, Island Life Photography

Sea turtle.
Photo courtesy of Dolphin Quest

What is a Dugong?

A dugong is a marine mammal and a relative of the manatee. Stories about the dugong may have started the folklore of mermaids.

3

Where Does A Marine Educator Work?

Marine educators work at aquariums, zoos, adventure parks, environmental organizations, or for the government. Many zoos are run by either the state or city government, and teach about both marine life and land animals. Aquariums also usually have marine education departments. In addition, the federal government has marine research and dolphin training programs through branches such as the Navy. Some aquarium educators and marine researchers work on boats and ships, and some even work on private tour boats. Marine educators work all over the world. One might think that all marine educators work near the ocean, but many work in aquariums far from it!

Tammy hanging out with her pal, Hoku. *Photo courtesy of Dolphin Quest*

Just chatting.
Photo courtesy of Dolphin Quest

Meet A Marine Educator!

Tammy Rach

Tammy has worked in the education departments at the Minnesota Zoo, the Aquarium of the Pacific, the San Diego Zoo's Wild Animal Park, and the Los Angeles Zoo.

Tammy cuddles with dolphin Kai Nalu.
Photo courtesy of Dolphin Quest

Pinnipeds

Seals, sea lions, and walruses are pinnipeds. Pinnipeds are finfooted, semi-aquatic marine mammals that can conserve oxygen for long periods of time underwater.

Meet Tammy Rach, a marine educator who has worked for many years at several zoos and aquariums. Tammy grew up in Minnesota and was more familiar with snowstorms than rainbows. As a young girl, she dreamed of someday working with dolphins, and her dream came true. During her career, Tammy has been a Marine Education Supervisor in Hawaii, where she was able to enjoy amazing mountains, palm trees, flowers, and ocean views. As a marine educator, she has worked not only with dolphins, but with all different types of marine life, including fish and invertebrates. One of her favorite parts of her marine career has been training seals and sea lions.

Differences Between Seals and Sea Lions:

True seals don't have external ear flaps like humans. Instead, they hear through holes in the sides of their heads. Meanwhile, sea lions have small external ear flaps that poke out from the sides of their heads.

True seals have short front flippers that help them steer in the water. Sea lions use their larger front flippers to propel themselves through the water and to "walk" on land.

The biggest difference between seals and sea lions is how they use their rear flippers: sea lions use their rear flippers to shuffle along on land. True seals use their rear flippers to help them swim. On land, these hind flippers trail behind them; they move by bouncing along on their bellies.

Seal pup on the beach.
Photo courtesy of Jessica Aschettino, Island Life Photography

Sea lion enjoying a swim.
Photo courtesy of PhotoDisc, Inc.

Organizing Learning Events

Kids pretend to be stingrays by using their "ampullae of Lorenzini electroreceptors" to scan the ocean floor for fish.
Photo courtesy of Tammy Rach

Marine educators often organize special learning events such as summer camps. Tammy loves creating programs from scratch, making up creative and fun ways to capture imaginations and help people understand the lives of marine animals. In one of Tammy's programs, kids use metal detectors to scan the sandy beach for hidden metallic fish; they pretend to be stingrays using electromagnetic sensory organs to find their prey.

In another program, kids learn all about animal sounds. Tammy shares different animal sounds, and the children try to repeat them. The kids then put on stethoscope earpieces and place the opposite end in the water to hear amazing underwater sounds. Sound travels up to five times faster underwater than on land, so the kids hear a lot! They are able to hear fish, rays, sea stars, and other marine life.

Art is used as a teaching tool. Here kids paint T-shirts with glow-in-the-dark paint. Some marine animals, like lanternfish and firefly squid, actually glow in the dark!
Photo courtesy of Tammy Rach

Workshops

Tammy during a classroom visit.
Photo courtesy of Tasha Jacobson

How Would You Like To Sleep Next To a Shark?

Occasionally, organizations will host sleepover educational programs for children.

A sleepover event.
Photo courtesy of Tasha Jacobson

Sometimes marine educators visit schools or put on workshops for groups that range in age from preschool to adult teachers. Tammy visits schools to provide information, provoke curiosity, and teach games and activities that educate about wildlife habitat, marine life, and conservation issues.

Internship Programs

Most marine educators create and run volunteer and/or internship programs to teach interested students more about the field. Tammy teaches interns over the age of sixteen. Volunteering is one way to learn about marine education as a career.

Interns training.
Photo courtesy of Dolphin Quest

Volunteer and intern duties vary depending on the facility, its needs, and what opportunities are available. Some zoos and aquariums have education volunteers who take classes to learn about specific animals and how to teach people about them. These volunteers may work at animal touch labs or informational booths and give presentations. Some aquariums have marine mammal volunteers who clean exhibits, prepare animal diets, and sometimes even help train animals. There are also dive volunteers who have experience diving in a variety of scenarios. They donate their time to help clean exhibits, feed animals underwater, and may give presentations underwater in special masks. And many internships offer the opportunity for students to do some or all of these things, helping trainers, educators, aquarists, and more. No matter what program volunteers donate their time and talents to, they gain invaluable experience, and their efforts are greatly appreciated.

Interns have a hands-on session with dolphin Hoku.
Photo courtesy of Dolphin Quest

Writing

Marine educators also usually write educational materials. Some write informational packets, handouts, and articles for newsletters. Others write brochures, teacher resource activity books, Web site information, or intern training material. Many write complete educational programs.

For example, before conducting a school program, educators often create a Pre-Program Materials packet to send to the teacher. This may include background information and interactive activities, as well as experiments and games for the teacher to do with the class before an aquarium educator visits.

Tammy Writes

• Activity and animal information brochures
• Teacher activity books
• New educational programs
• Articles in newsletters for staff, teachers, and program participants

Tammy at work, writing programs.
Photo courtesy of Ruth Bonomo

This packet helps students start to learn the basics about the topic of the program. Then during the school visit, the educator brings objects to the classroom that the teacher may not have access to, like marine mammal bones, models of coral, or even expensive equipment. After the visit is complete, the educator leaves a Post-Program Materials packet to help the teacher continue on with the lessons learned. It often takes a great deal of time and research for an educator to create the perfect program curriculum for each age group. Marine educators often send their written programs to teachers and marine educators at other places for testing, editing, and to receive suggestions for improvement.

Tammy has written educational programs, resources for teachers, tour guide monologues, classes, shows, and presentations.

check it out!

Visit www.dolphinquest.org to find some materials that Tammy and other marine educators have worked on, including a brochure called "Careers Working With Marine Animals." This site also contains more marine animal information, as well as several learning games.

Adventure Programs

Tammy enjoys creating learning, adventure, and investigatory programs for children. Every program she creates is filled with fun. Here are some of the activities Tammy plans:

Feeding Frenzy

While eating a picnic lunch, the kids observe how different animals eat and then try to replicate the different feeding strategies they observe. They also compare and contrast their hands, mouth, teeth, and utensils to the different feeding adaptations other animals have. In one game, kids hold different kinds of "beaks" (long, thin beaks, large, scoop beaks, etc.) in one hand, and mock "stomachs" in the other hand. Then a variety of "food" objects is tossed onto the ground. The kids try to pick up the food using various bird beaks to see which beaks work best for which types of food. For example, birds like egrets use their long, chopstick-like beaks to reach down quickly and grab slippery fish. Pelicans, on the other hand, use their larger beaks to scoop up fish.

A dolphin (Liho) investigates.
Photo courtesy of Dolphin Quest

Echolocation

Echolocation is a sensory sonar system used for communication and locating things in the environment.

Using echolocation, dolphins let out a series of clicking sounds. When the clicks strike an object, an echo bounces back, giving the dolphins a mental picture of their physical surroundings. Using echolocation, dolphins can determine the size and shape of an object, the direction it is traveling, its speed, how far away it is, and much more.

Dolphins play with familiar toys.
Photo courtesy of Dolphin Quest

Dockside Playtime

During dockside playtime, children observe how animals learn through play. The dolphins especially enjoy playing with basketballs, pool noodles, pool mats, and hula hoops. One activity the dolphins like is finding toys that are tossed in the water without using their eyes—they wear "eye cups" as blindfolds. The dolphins are able to find their toys not with their eyes, but by scanning using echolocation.

Kids find clues during a
mystery game.
Photo courtesy of Tammy Rach

Mammals

are animals that
breathe air using
lungs, nurse their
young with milk, have
hair, have a constant
temperature, and give
birth to live young.

Marine Mammals

comprise a diverse
group of about 120
species of mammals
that are primarily
ocean-dwelling or
depend on the ocean
for food. They live in
salt water, although
some will travel into
estuaries or freshwater
bays to catch fish.
Seals are examples of
marine mammals.

Try This
At Home!

Games With Marine Mammal Mysteries To Solve

Each game Tammy creates leads to a fun and exciting discovery. One game teaches the difference between how we make sounds (by vibrating our vocal cords) and how a dolphin makes sounds (by manipulating air sacs beneath its blowhole). A dolphin breathes and emits sounds using the hole on top of its head, called a blowhole. To demonstrate this concept, Tammy takes an un-inflated balloon and fills it with air, comparing it to the air sacs under a dolphin's blowhole. When air is released from the balloon, it squeaks and makes different sounds, similar to the sounds coming from air sacs below a dolphin's blowhole.

humpback whale's blowholes

dolphin's blowhole

Signature Whistle

As calves, bottlenose dolphins develop their own unique whistle, which they use throughout their lives to distinguish themselves from one another. These whistles can be compared to the naming system humans use. Just like we all have our own names, bottlenose dolphins each have their own signature whistles.

Communication

Ocean water can be dark and murky, so dolphins use sound to communicate with each other and to keep track of each other. They may also whistle when they discover potential prey, or when in distress.

How Many Blowholes?

Toothed whales, like the dolphin, have one blowhole while baleen whales, like the humpback whale, have two.

Close Encounters With Hawaiian Reef Fish, Green Sea Turtles, and Dolphins

When Tammy has children touch and feed animals up close, it makes a lasting impression on them. This hands-on approach allows for an immediate connection with the animals. They also learn about animal adaptations, including: coloration, eating adaptations, and defense strategies.

Adaptation: modification of an organism or its parts that makes it more fit for existence under the conditions of its environment.

Adaptation Examples:

Eating adaptation: Sea horses do not have teeth, so they suck up food with their snout and swallow it whole.

Defense strategy adaptation: Some fish have a false eye spot on or near their tails to confuse predators.

Coloration adaptation: Bottlenose dolphins have counter shading, which means their color is darker on top of their bodies and lighter underneath their bodies. This helps them blend in with their surroundings; this camouflage helps them hide from predators and also allows them to sneak up on prey.

Dive Deeper

Dolphins have teeth, but do they chew their food?

No, they swallow it whole! They use their teeth to catch fish and squid.

Adaptation: modification of an organism or its parts that makes it more fit for existence under the conditions of its environment

Adaptation Examples:
* Eating adaptation
* Defense strategy adaptation
* Coloration adaptation

Dolphin time with trainer
Jessica Aschettino.
Photo courtesy of Tammy Rach

When seen from above, a dolphin's darker shade on top blends in with the dark water. When viewed from below, the lighter color blends in with the surface of the ocean, which is lighter.

A parent and child participate in a Wee Family, Fins, and Fun program.
Photo courtesy of Dolphin Quest

Who Do Marine Educators Work With?

Conference for educators of the Alliance of Marine Mammal Parks and Aquariums.
Photo provided by Tammy Rach

Marine educators usually work with trainers, other department managers, curators, volunteers, students, aquarists, and guest services staff. Tammy works with all of these, but mostly she works with volunteers, students, and the public. She also has close working relationships with the aquarists and trainers. In addition, Tammy has met with marine educators from Mexico, the Bahamas, Denmark, Bermuda, Japan, and many more places around the world.

Marine educators from around the world. Educators at an Alliance of Marine Mammal Parks and Aquariums Educators meeting.
Photo provided by Tammy Rach

Do Marine Educators Travel?

Tammy and Robyn Larkin participating in a sea turtle catch and release research project in Bermuda.
Photo courtesy of Dolphin Quest

Some educators may travel for conferences or new learning opportunities. Many enjoy traveling to participate in conservation projects. Tammy has traveled to Baja to release sea turtles tagged with satellite trackers. This kind of equipment helps scientists learn more about animals in the wild: how they move, where they go, and why. Tammy has also participated in a sea turtle research project in Bermuda, where young sea turtles were collected, measured, weighed, tagged, and released.

Hanauma Bay, the Island of Oahu.
Photo courtesy of Melissa Malmstedt

This information helps researchers learn about the health of turtles in certain areas and how we can protect them. Tammy has also been to many conferences with other marine educators. For example, she has traveled to Florida, Alabama, Georgia, and Hawaii to meet with marine educators from around the world to share and exchange information.

Conservation

If you love marine life, you want to protect it. Marine educators do their part to protect the environment, and they teach others about the importance of conservation.

One game Tammy has kids play is called the "Recycle Relay." The kids take a large bag of trash and, while racing in teams, sort through it, dividing it into items that can be recycled, re-used, or left in the trash. In the end, most of the trash is put into the recycle or re-use piles. Cans, bottles, milk jugs, cell phones, water bottles, paper, newspaper, fishing line, batteries, boxes, cardboard, and glass can *all* be recycled. Re-using and recycling is important because the trash that we throw away stays for a long time in landfills and on our planet—sometimes for hundreds, thousands, and even millions of years!

What is Conservation?

Conservation is the protection and safe-keeping of the environment, wildlife, and natural resources. Some well-known conservation organizations include: Ocean Conservancy, The Nature Conservancy, World Wildlife Fund, and Natural Resource Defense Council.

Decomposition:
to rot or break up

How quickly some common items decompose:
* Paper: 2-4 weeks
* Banana peel: up to 2 years
* Wool sock: 1-5 years
* Disposable diaper: 10-20 years
* Plastic bag: 10-20 years
* Aluminum can: 80-100 years
* Plastic six-pack soda can holder: 100 years
* Glass: up to a million years
* Styrofoam: never. It breaks down into smaller pieces, but it does not degrade or turn into dirt—it stays styrofoam.

Dangerous Litter

Turtles often mistake plastic bags for sea jellies and when they try to eat the bags, they can get sick and some even die.

Tammy also explains that when garbage is not disposed of properly, it has a good chance of ending up in the water somewhere. Even the balloons that float away eventually fall down and end up in the water! Marine animals can choke on these balloons and other refuse that they try to eat, and if they swallow it, it can block their digestive tracts.

The choices we make every day affect our world. Marine educators want kids to know that everyone can make a difference, whether they live by the ocean or not! Recycle and re-use objects whenever you can.

Sea turtle release off of the Kahala Beach at Dolphin Quest.
Photo courtesy of Tammy Rach

Beach Clean-Ups

International
Coastal Clean-up
at Hanauma Bay.
*Photo provided by
Tammy Rach*

*That's A
Bunch of
Trash!*

Tammy and
her crew find
loads of trash,
including:
plastic, nets,
cans, plastic
bottles, rope,
balloons, ribbons,
and buoys—all of
which can be
harmful to
marine life.

Marine educators are usually conservation-minded and participate in programs to help the environment. Tammy and her staff participate in beach clean-ups in order to help keep marine environments clean for their animal inhabitants, and to set a good example for others. Many animals die each year because they accidentally eat or are entangled in trash. Some beach clean-ups, like the International Coastal Cleanup, actually count each trash item and collect data from around the world. The data collected helps scientists determine what the main pollution problems are in the ocean, and what needs to be fixed or changed to help the environment. Marine educators are passionate about conservation and love to help save habitats and animals however they can.

Other conservation programs include: marine research, invasive algae removal, coral reef surveys, and more.

Jan and Tammy digging in bushes for trash in an effort to clean up the beach.
Photo provided by Tammy Rach

Habitats

There are many different beautiful and amazing habitats in the ocean, such as coral reefs, kelp forests, deep water trenches, sea grass beds, and more. A habitat is an ecological or environmental area that is inhabited by particular species. Coral reefs are usually found in warm, shallow waters; tropical coral thrives in lots of sunlight. Kelp forest beds are usually in more mild waters where currents bring nutrient-rich waters. There are also different layers of ocean water, such as the sunlit zone near the shore, the twilight zone, and the midnight zone.

Whale Watching

As part of her job, Tammy also studies Oahu's humpback whale population by hiking with a team to a special whale-watching area and recording the number of adult and calf whales sighted and their behaviors over four-hour time periods. The data collected appears in the community newspaper. The purpose of the count is to increase community awareness and appreciation of the humpback whale population. Hopefully, this awareness encourages the community to take care to protect endangered humpback whales, as well as other natural resources.

Tammy Counts

- Breaches: more than 2/3 of the humpback whale's body has to come out of the water to be considered a breach
- Tail Slaps: a slap of the tail on the water
- Blows: an exhale out of the blowhole(s)

Whale watching at Ka'ena Point West.
Photo courtesy of Tammy Rach

A whale's fluke held in the air as it dives.
Photo courtesy of Jessica Aschettino, Island Life Photography

A whale calf breaches the surface.
Photo courtesy of Jessica Aschettino, Island Life Photography

Working Conditions

Tammy at work
on a boat.
*Photo courtesy of
Robyn Larkin*

Marine educators can work in a variety of environments, depending on who they work for. Most work both inside and outside, often in all sorts of weather.

Sometimes, they even get wet! You will find marine educators working in classrooms, aquariums, zoos, in theaters, on boats, and on the beach. Spending so much time outdoors may be uncomfortable for some people. Marine educators may have to deal with extreme weather, sunburn, and chills from being in the water much of the time.

Tammy working in the water and on a sunny beach.
Photos courtesy of Dolphin Quest

Marine Educators and Their Tools

Marine educators use many tools to perform their jobs. A marine educator uses a computer, as well as copy machines, a desk, file cabinets, carts to haul supplies around, and sometimes even a company truck or boat!

Some wear a company uniform, which might be a swimming suit. Tammy wears a rash guard (a thin, short- or long-sleeved shirt) to protect herself from the sun and from sea jelly stings.

Tammy in her rash guard.
Photo courtesy of Tammy Rach

Tools of the Trade

Beyond office supplies like computers, Tammy also uses a sewing machine to make costumes, bags, and curtains. She makes programs and activities using craft supplies like foam, glue, stickers, glow-in-the-dark gel pens, and googly eyes for little critters.

Education and Skills Needed

Tammy teaching a preschool class.
Photo courtesy of Dolphin Quest

Most marine educators have a four-year college degree. Some have more advanced degrees as well. A background in science and good training in communication skills will help prepare you for a career in marine education.

It is also helpful to have: teaching experience, customer service experience, curriculum development skills, and computer knowledge. Tammy says that lots of energy and the ability to think creatively are also important.

Opportunities!

The experience and education marine educators acquire can lead to flexible career opportunities. For example, Tammy has worked in education departments at both zoos and aquariums. Currently, she is the Senior Volunteer Manager at the San Diego Zoo.

Interested In a Marine Education Career?

The best thing to do if you are interested in becoming a marine educator is to learn all that you can about marine life and get as much experience as you can.

Learn and Get Experience!

* First, read all about marine life, everywhere you can. Visit aquariums and zoos, and ask questions.
* Research marine life and share what you've learned with your class, family, or friends.
* Join a zoo, aquarium class, or camp.
* Ask to help clean parks with your family.
* Try taking care of your own aquarium of tropical fish, but make sure to purchase your fish from responsible sources to avoid threatened or endangered species.
* Gain hands-on experience with all sorts of animals.

Dolphins love to be loved.
Photo courtesy of Dolphin Quest

Tip From Tammy

"Hands-on experience is like gold ... start volunteering as soon as you're old enough. Zoos, aquariums, and rescue/rehab shelters all usually need volunteers."

Try This:

Experiment #1:

Fill several plastic containers (such as clean yogurt or margarine tubs) with various substances such as rice, pebbles, sand, or other small objects that would make noise when shaken. Be careful to place only one type of item in each container. Have friends fill their plastic containers with other objects. Exchange canisters and shake each other's "mystery sounds" to test how well you hear by sound alone. Try to find a match when the same objects are shaken. This experiment helps illustrate how dolphins communicate, each with its own signature sound.

Experiment #2:

Vibrating bones: Put your left hand over your left ear with your elbow sticking straight ahead. Hold a tuning fork on the single spoke between your right thumb and index finger, and tap one of the double spokes on something hard. Place the ball of the tuning fork directly on the bone in your elbow.

What do you hear? These are sound waves traveling through your bones; they are similar to sound waves that bounce back through a dolphin's lower jaw bone when it uses echolocation. Even though the dolphin's jaw is hollow, fluid-filled, and much more sensitive than your bones, the way you are "hearing" the vibrations is similar.

You can experiment with the tuning fork and sound traveling through your bones by placing your elbow on your knee and then tapping the tuning fork on your toe, your shin, etc. Experiment—it's fun!

Note: Tuning forks are available at music, teacher supply, or education-related stores.

Where Can I Learn More?

Career Options

If a career in Marine Education interests you, you may also want to consider a career as a:
• Researcher
• Field Biologist
• Animal Caregiver
• Veterinarian
• Whale Watch Guide
• Conservationist
• Marine Artist, Illustrator, Writer, Designer, or Filmmaker

Teaching others about marine life is an important job. In order for people to appreciate nature, they need to understand it and care about it. Marine educators bring awareness of the ocean and its creatures to others. It is important to understand that everything we do impacts the environment and ocean, and marine educators help people understand that. Maybe someday you will have a career in marine education! Check out the following organizations to learn more about it:

Organizations

Alliance of Marine Mammal Parks and Aquariums (AMMPA)
www.ammpa.org
ammpa@aol.com

Association of Zoos and Aquariums
www.aza.org
8403 Colesville Road, Suite 710, Silver Spring, MD 20910
(301) 562-0777

National Marine Educators Association
www.marine-ed.org
703 East Beach Dr., Ocean Springs, MS 39564
(228) 818-8893

Dolphin Quest Oahu
www.dolphinquest.org
5000 Kahala Avenue, Honolulu, HI 96816
(808) 739-8918

A sea turtle released at Kahala Beach.
Photo courtesy of Tammy Rach

Web Sites

www.afsc.noaa.gov This site has information about marine animals and marine mammal careers under the marine mammal education section.

www.oceansforyouth.org This is an educational site for kids of all ages.

www.coralfilm.com This site has a coral reef adventure fun zone. It's a great place to learn about the various plants and animals that live in coral reefs.

www.pbs.org/oceanrealm This site looks at unique creatures of the ocean.

www.aquariumofpacific.org Check out the online learning center under the education section to understand the diversity of marine life and habitats.

www.seaworld.org Learn about animal species found around the world.

www.mbayaq.org This site has games and activities, as well as information on science careers.

Books

Cool Careers for Girls with Animals, by Ceel Pasternak and Linda Thornburg.

Dolphin Man: Exploring the World of Dolphins, by Laurence Pringle.

Dolphins, by Jason Skog.

Oceans: An Activity Guide for Ages 6-9, by Nancy Castaldo.

Opportunities in Marine and Maritime Careers, by William Ray Heitzmann.

Secrets of the Dolphins, by K.C. Kelley.

Working with Wildlife: A Guide to Careers in the Animal World, by Thane Maynard.

Tammy loves sea turtles!
Photo courtesy of Robyn Larkin